Zero BS Estate A[

The Zero Bullshit Guide to Selling Your
Home For The Highest Net Profit in a
Timeframe You Control With An Agent
You Can Trust...

Introduction

In Estate Agency, there are three types of Estate Agent.

Professional, unethical and the 'Dishonourable.

The 'Dishonourables' are people that lack courage to do what's right and equally... they lack the skill to mould and shape the perfect sale for their clients.

No courage. No guts. Preferring to rely on hope and crossed fingers to sell houses.

Worse, these people take zero responsibility for non-action.

They're literally glorified attendants too scared to tell you what they really think just in case they miss out on winning your instruction.

Why...?

Because keeping their office doors open is more important than doing what's right, and only interested in selling lengthy contracts, not houses.

Worse, if lady luck isn't on their side, they drift off, leaving you to fend for yourself…

…which will cost you thousands of pounds...

These agents are unskilled. They lack talent or the resourcefulness to deliver everything they said they would.

Further, if they end up agreeing a sale, the process from offer accepted to completing will be a painful process.

The Unethicals
The 'Unethicals' on the other hand know exactly what they're doing!

They understand how to take advantage of you...

They understand the allure of 'stars in your eyes' valuations…

They know how hard it is for sellers to resist the temptation of a huge valuation.

Make no mistake. These guys are skilled. Very skilled. They are incredible salesmen in the art of bullshitting made to look sincere, honest, and full of integrity…

What these charlatans are selling actually though, is snake oil, elixirs and dreams.

And this type of agent everyone is in on the act from the receptionist to the CEO.

It's all part of their plan.

Here's how it works.

The 'Unethicals' will arrange as many viewings as they can. It doesn't matter whether a buyer asked to see your home or not. The buyer was being taken there anyway.

This is to make it look like the agent is working hard for you and because there's no offers, the only option is to reduce the initial asking price. And again. And again, until finally you accept a below market value offer…

The 'unethicals' are concerned with making sales to fulfil their financial dreams and using your property to hit their goals.

Said differently, the price they suggested they knew you would never achieve in the first place…

Honestly, these people are wolves in sheep's clothing and would steal the eyes out of your head if you weren't looking.

The problem for you.

To sell your home for what you really deserve, you don't have a second chance to make a first impression.

These agents know this.

But…

They also know that if they tell you the truth of what your property is really worth, they know the race to winning your instruction will be a level playing field amongst their peer group of competing agents.

Your life.

Your journey.

Your next chapter…

Isn't of any concern to them.

They don't care.

Showing you how to truly maximise the real value of your home is the last thing on their agenda.

Instead, they deliberately chose tactics and strategies that cost homeowners thousands of pounds in lost revenue on the real value of their home's.

What I'm going to say may sting you a little.

The truth is.

Sellers more often than not, go with the agent that gave the highest marketing figure and disregard the agent who said the least. They assume the agent who said the least doesn't know their market.

And in the end, the lowest priced agent is accused of trying to undersell to one of his developer mates or sell cheap to make a quick buck…

Thing is…

Achieving the highest net profit is the easy part when it comes to selling your home. But it's also the foundation of creating a sale you're in control of…

So how do you tell the difference between the professionals, dishonourables and unethicals?

In this eBook, I'm gonna reveal to you exactly how…

…the rest is in your hands.

MY 10 PROPERTY SELLING TENETS

TRUTH #1 - AN ESTATE AGENT IS A RENTED ASSET AND LIKE ANY PIECE OF RENTED EQUIPMENT, IF IT'S NOT PERFORMING MAKE SURE IT CAN BE HANDED BACK WITHOUT PENALTY

TRUTH #2 – IT'S NOT THE PROMISE OF A PRICE THAT ACHIEVES THE HIGHEST NET PROFIT. IT'S THE PROCESS

TRUTH #3 - PROPERTY IS NOT IN ISOLATION. IT'S IN COMPETITION

TRUTH #4 – A PROPERTY THAT IS WORTH WHAT SOMEONE IS WILLING TO PAY FOR IT, IS WORTH MORE TO COMPETING BUYERS

TRUTH #5 - RIGHT SYSTEM + RIGHT SALESPEOPLE = OUTSTANDING SUCCESS

TRUTH #6 - BUYERS ARE MORE MOTIVATED BY WHAT THEY WILL NOT BE ABLE TO GET IF THEY DONT BUY NOW

TRUTH #7 - HIRE RIGHT, BECAUSE THE PENALTIES FOR HIRING WRONG COSTS THOUSANDS

TRUTH #8 - ALL PROPERTIES ARE DIFFERENT. DON'T TREAT THEM THE SAME. TREAT THEM APPROPRIATELY

TRUTH #10 - AGENTS ARE NOT THE EMPLOYER. SELLERS ARE

Forward...

Despite the best efforts of the selling solicitor trying to ruin the sale, the seller and I ended up becoming good friends.

So much so, she recommended me to a friend who was about to sell.

Just one issue.

The flat was 6.7 miles up the road in Colindale and what did I know about Colindale?

I was selling property in Ladbroke Grove.

I didn't know anything about the schools in Colindale. The transport links in Colindale. The shops in Colindale . I had nothing to go on. I didn't even know where the flat was.

I couldn't help.

But Mark (the seller), was having none of my insecurities and wouldn't accept no for an answer.

A bit of background about Mark's flat.

Firstly, the flat had a short lease which was valued at £28,000 to extend.

Not only that. At £100 per square foot, the refurb was going to cost around £40,000.

My other problem.

I wouldn't be able to get the time off work to sell it. So I needed to find an agency in Colindale that could.

But would my method of selling property work in a different location? I didn't know as I had never done something like this before...

So I went about discovering the wheat from the chaff and found 8 agents operating in Colindale.

Admittedly, I was panicking. What if I didn't find an agent I could rely on? What if I failed?

I needed to understand who they were and what they stood for? I wanted to know what motivated them?

I didn't care at this stage if they were horrible dirty lying cheats. Or whether they were nobelist of knights.

The only thing I was interested in, wasn't just how honest they were and how they came to their assumption(s). I also wanted to know their plan.

Some of the responses I got from agents went from astonishing at one end of the bullsh*t scale to perplexing at the other end.

One had a great start introducing himself and company. But got agitated when I asked questions.

How on earth would he cope when things get tough during the sale?

Others were selling me fluff talking up the market. and if the market was as good as they were saying, great. They just had to prove it. If the market was bad, they had to show me why it was bad. If there were a lack of buyers, I wanted them to say so.

Of the 8 agents I spoke to. 3 were invited over to value the flat.

The first agent bored the hell out of me. It wasn't that he wasn't a good guy. I just questioned whether he actually wanted to be there... No drive. No determination.

He worried me...

That said, I was Impressed with the second agent until he said, "I'd tell 'em (buyers) what I need to, to get a deal through...!"

The last agent, Ronald (Andrews Online in Kingsbury) was a complete professional.

Brutally honest and incredibly professional.

His pitch was all about his agency's method of how to maximise the value of their client's property. I loved it.

He got the instruction...

After two weeks of marketing, Ronald arranged 17 viewings and achieved 5 offers.

Eventually, he agreed the sale at £248,000 from a marketing price of £225,000...!

To put how good this was into perspective...

The best flat on the street that had all the bells and whistles. Decent interior. Long lease etc sold for £265,000.

Mark's flat that needed a £28,000 lease extension including £40,000 worth of refurbishment work.

The reality. Mark's flat should have sold for £200,000...

Why am I telling you this story...?

If homeowners looked at agents like they were candidates interviewing for a business they had just set up. Homeowners would discover the professionals amongst the charlatans.

In other words, I'm gonna give you the questions that reveal the agents that are highly skilled with the track record to back it up.

In other words …

I'm showing you how to spot the difference between the good (pro's), the bad (Dishonourables) and the ugly (The Unethicals…)

Said differently, if you're the type of seller that wants to be represented by an agent who delivers results so you can choose what the next chapter in your life looks like, continue reading…

"MY PROMISE TO YOU…"

My last boss said to me, "Surely if a house is worth £500,000. You'd say £550,000 to get the client?"

"NO! NO! and F**KING NO AGAIN WILL I SAY SOMETHING JUST TO WIN AN INSTRUCTION BASED ON BULLSHIT!!!"

Where was my tribe? Why can't I keep my feelings in check? Why does bullsh*t affect me so much? Why can't I just fall in line?

When I presented how to achieve maximum money for homeowners, all I got back was blank stares…

The best my colleagues could offer, *"Homeowners out here won't accept the London way of doing business!"*

You couldn't make this sh*t up.

Not too long after, I was instructed on a three-bedroom detached, albeit located in a floodplain. eek…

That said, my method (Highest Net Profit Formula) generated 41 enquiries within days of going live on the market.

From those enquiries, we block booked 17 viewings with buyers that were likely to offer.

Up to that point, my colleagues had never seen buyer urgency like this!

My client had bought this house for £530,000 eight months earlier and at the time of the sale, we were in a falling market…

When we agreed the sale 2 weeks later, not only did I pay for myself (agency fees), but the extra money also paid for her solicitor fees, removal costs etc…

"F**k You!" I thought to myself…

In the end, I sold my clients property for £30,000 than she paid for it.

Despite this, I was quickly losing faith in this industry.

I hated the industry for what it stood for.

I hated the people in it.

I hated the lack of consequences agents didn't face if they failed to deliver on their promises.

I hated the lack of truth.

But worse than anything, I hated myself because I had neither the money nor the resources to continue the fight against unethical and Dishonourable estate agents.

I had lost all hope of making a meaningful impact in this industry.

Until now…

My promise to you…

If you ask the questions inside this book to every single agent you invite to value your home, not only will you maximise the value of your home…

You will put yourself in complete and total control of the sale of your property…

Not at the mercy of an agent that couldn't care about your future or how you get there…

The rest is up to you.

"HOW TO USE THIS BOOK..."

In the following chapters, you will discover the '21 Secret Insider Questions' the unethicals and dishonourable agents do not want you to know.

The '21 Secret Insider Questions' shows whether an agent has a delivery format that suits your property. Whether they work to deadlines and or project milestones/goals so you know what part of the journey you're on.

The '21 Secret Insider Questions' will reveal the agent's company mission, vision and philosophy AND OR whether they have one?

I'll show you how surveyors think.

You'll also discover why the agent with all the glitz, glamour and the most local instructions can't be trusted...

The '21 SECRET INSIDER QUESTIONS' are written in specific order to ensure that by the end of the valuation process, you're employing an agent that has a strategy to achieve the highest net profit for your home (in any market).

They are my cheat sheet to continually monitor the agent you've instructed is providing the highest level of service they possibly could.

In your hands right now is the power to truly discover the very best agents that know exactly how to maximise the value of your home…

To your success…

INSIDER QUESTION #1

"If you win my instruction, how much do you suggest we market my property for...?"

The answer is not about how many magazines or portals the agent promises to put your property.

Superior marketing means shit if the price is wrong..

Seriously, get the price wrong and you can kiss goodbye what you want to happen in your next property chapter of your life...

Tom Panos, one of Australia's most well-respected agents said recently, "*If you go too high on the price, you'll have an overpriced turkey and the owner would say, "you told me that you would get me that price!"*"

He went on, "*But if you say exactly what it's worth, most of the time, it's lower than what the owner wants...*"

Panos explains there are three figures when selling: The *Emotional, The Probable and The Mathematical.*

"The *Emotional* price is where someone falls in love with your home and would do anything to get it. Or for example, the neighbour that has just split with her partner. She has a 5-year-old (and with parents that'll help financially), they'll pay more for your home than a general buyer.

Relies on a relationship breaking down.

Not a good strategy right.

"Then there's the *Probable* figure. This is the figure based on comparable evidence of other similar properties that have sold for. This is where surveyors working on behalf of banks operate.

They'll only be interested in sold prices within the last 6 months for properties similar to yours within a 1 mile radius.

No proof, the surveyor won't sign it off and the bank won't be lending your buyer the money to buy your home.

"*And the third figure is the Mathematical figure…*" Panos states, "*Buyers at this level are where bargain hunters operate*".

In other words, marketing your property at the emotional figure, you'll only end up attracting bargain basement offers.

Why?

Because buyers won't buy what other buyers don't want…

INSIDER QUESTION #2

"What Percentage of Asking Price Do You Achieve on Average For Your Seller's...?"

The closer to 100% of their original suggested asking price an Agent is, the more integrity they have.

This is the easiest question to answer of all the 21 questions if the agents you're talking to really do put their clients first...

An agent that on average achieves 95% and below, you're speaking with a snake oils salesman. 96% is the UK average (aka shockingly bad). 97% is above the national average but nowhere close to being okay. 98% valuation accuracy is heading in the right direction and 99% equates to massive levels of integrity and professionalism.

My current average is 99.47%

So when an agent tells you how well their agency is performing and how they've sold more than any other agent in the local area.

All that's great.

But if their valuation accuracy rate is 96%

Are they the type of agent that would fight for every penny your property deserves or are they only interested in selling you a lengthy contract?

The point I'm making…

No matter how nice an agent's word's sound, their numbers speak for themselves.

The closer to 100% valuation accuracy rate the better they perform and the better your selling journey will be.

The further away from 100% equates to a lack of skill, knowledge and integrity…

INSIDER QUESTION #3

"How many days are your properties on the market before they go under offer...?"

No word of a lie, you should be under offer within 30 days of coming to market.

An agent's sole aim should be deliberately positioning your property to attract as many ready, willing and able buyers as possible to compete for your home.

The UK average of days on market is 168 days!

Like WTF!!

1 day beyond 30 days, there better be a good reason.

But 168 days and beyond, you're speaking with an agent that doesn't know what they're doing or the more likely version, they're knowingly locking you into a 60 to 200 day sole agency contract you can't get out of.

But why is 30 days the benchmark?

Because to the buying public, a property sitting on the market for longer than 30 looks like there could be something wrong with it.

Remember, you don't get a second chance to make a first impression when your home goes to market.

Property that does go under offer within 30 days of coming to market, isn't priced cheap. It's priced right and more importantly, puts you in control of the selling journey, not the bargain hunters looking to prey on the potentially vulnerable...

INSIDER QUESTION #4

"What has your VIEWING to OFFER ratio been in the last 12 months...?"

When I first started in this industry, I showed buyers what they asked to go and see.

Sounds normal right.

You want to go and see a property, I'll show you.

Thing is…

That got me more complaints than offers...

Literally, buyers complained to my manager that I was showing them the wrong properties.

"But how could I be!?" I would ask.

THEY ASKED TO SEE WHAT I SHOWED THEM!

The truth is, I didn't know what I was doing...

Said differently, if you were a client of mine, you would have been spending ages making your home look pristine for buyers that had little to no intention of purchasing your home.

I literally didn't qualify buyers good enough and was letting my sellers down.

Fact is, every buyer an agent brings to view your home should be coming with a view to making you an offer…

Today, I point blank refuse to show a buyer a property if they're not right for it.

But what if an agency is bringing Tom, Dick and Harry deliberately?

How would you really know in advance that this is their business model designed to get you to reduce later…

The beauty of question #4, is that you now know, every buyer an agent brings to your home should be coming with a view to making you an offer.

If they don't offer, why?

And if the agency doesn't know what their viewing to offer ratio is…

That's because of 2 things…

1. The office negotiators don't know how to properly qualify buyers and are simply door openers…
2. It's part of the show, and all the agents inside the office are in on the act looking acting like they don't know why no one's offering

Either way…

Run.

INSIDER QUESTION #5

"How many properties have you been instructed to sell and how many of these have you completed on in the last 12 months...?"

According to Rightmove, a whooping 60% of sellers end up selling their home through the second agent!

Florent Lambert, Director of Estate Agency Home Domus 360 in Essex wrote is area, *"Across Essex I find that the average sale ratio over 12 months is about 40% but only about 15% of agents achieve a sale ratio over 50% and only about 3% over 65%*

Of purple bricks he said,"...despite taking the money early and therefore keeping their customers for longer, Purplebricks only achieve just over the average around 42-44% sale ratio over a 12 months period.

"The large corporate chains of estate agents do deliver a poor sale ratio, Bairstow Eves and Abbotts among the worst ones."

But in my experience, a seller deciding not to sell after going to market is rare.

Yes, things change.

Yes people decide not to sell for whatever reason.

But the reason so many property sales full through is because they were won based on lies and deceit, not integrity and professionalism.

Said differently…

Property doesn't fail to sell because sellers and buyers intentions change.

More often than not, it's because the agents set the sale, marketing and promotion completely wrong.

Remember, although agents wield great power in a property sale, they are still a very small cog in the property market.

And an agent can't be exact with you about how many instructions they win versus how many they sell, why don't they know their numbers?

My rolling average is almost 1 in 1.

INSIDER QUESTION #6

"How many properties have you sold at the asking price or above in the last 12 months...?"

Below are my marketing prices in the left green column vs. what I achieved in the right green column with the percentage achieved in the right-hand column.

47 Eynham Road	£ 485,000	£485,000.00	100.00
93 West Row	£ 349,950	£334,000.00	95.44
4 Malvern Close	£ 850,000	£850,000.00	100.00
20 Chesterton Road	£ 610,000	£615,000.00	100.82
12 Croft House	£ 300,000	295000.00	98.33
24 Lothrop Road	£ 775,000	£735,000.00	94.84
15a Eynham Road	£ 725,000	£725,000	100.00
61 Lancaster Road	£ 440,000	£420,000.00	95.45
12c St Marks Place	£ 280,000	£280,000.00	100.00
92 Cambridge Gardens	£ 550,000	£500,000.00	90.91
4 Nascot Street	£ 550,000	£525,000.00	95.45
84 Cambridge Gardens	£ 450,000	£450,000.00	100.00
25 Kilravock Street	£ 750,000	£715,000.00	95.33
166 Ladbroke Grove	£ 550,000	£550,000.00	100.00
59 Lowerwood Court	£ 325,000	£340,000.00	104.62
231 Ladbroke Grove	£ 275,000	£275,000.00	100.00
Pav Terrace	£ 499,999	£491,000.00	98.20

58 Noko	£ 460,000	£450,000.00	97.83
77 Noko	£ 410,000	£390,000.00	95.12
46 Noko	£ 420,000	£400,000.00	95.24
76 Noko	£ 420,000	£400,000.00	95.24
37 Noko	£ 395,000	£420,000.00	106.33
228 LG	£ 550,000	£540,000.00	98.18
33 Bartholomew House	£ 425,500	£422,500.00	99.29
15 James House	£ 375,000	£375,000.00	100.00
73 Bramley Road	£ 225,000	£251,750.00	111.89
1 James House	£ 385,000	£395,000.00	102.60
98h Cambridge Gardens	£ 450,000	£450,000.00	100.00
27 St Andrews	£ 730,000	£730,000.00	100.00
144 Kilburn Lane	£ 775,000	£750,000.00	96.77
Flat 3 40 Bassett Road	£ 690,000	£690,000.00	100.00
125 Ladbroke Grove	£ 650,000	£705,000.00	108.46
25 Bartholomew	£ 385,000	£410,000.00	106.49
59 Tavistock Cres	£ 425,000	£ 400,000	94.12
11 Noko	£ 460,000	£ 475,000	103.26
13 Noko	£ 460,000	£ 475,000	103.26
35 Noko	£ 500,000	£ 500,000	100.00
48 St Lawrence	£ 600,000	£ 617,000	102.83
345 347 Ladbroke Grove	£ 350,000	£353,000.00	100.86
F3 61 Lancaster Road	£450,000	£450,000.00	100.00
104 Lancaster Road	£ 685,000	£670,000.00	97.81
16 Bartholomew House	£ 500,000	£500,000.00	100.00

4 Garnet Court, Marlow	£ 535,000	£560,000.00	104.67

So why is question #6 important?

Because what sort of sale would you like when selling?

One where you're in control of your sale or one where days and weeks turn into months of sitting stagnant on the market?

The question to have in the back of your mind before you employ n agent to represent you... *"Is this agency attempting to deliberately position my property to attract the very best buyers to compete for my signature or are they just saying things that sound nice to win my instruction?"*

Because as you'll have just seen.

I don't always get it right.

The difference is, I will sell your home for free should I fail to deliver on my price promise.

INSIDER QUESTION #7

"Can you explain in detail what other properties similar to mine have sold for and when...?"

'What Agent's Want You To Believe When Selling Your Home...'

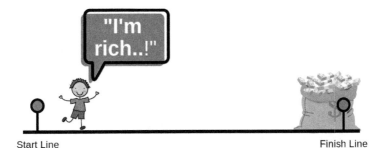

Start Line   Finish Line

In the illustration above, unethical and the dishonourable agents give the impression that the house selling journey is the easiest thing in the world.

Put the house on at the "Emotional Figure". Bob's your uncle. Fanny's ya Aunt. Bish Bash Bosh, job's a good'un. Sell for massive money and you don't even have to be good at it.

It's easy...

But... is this really the case?

Surveyors, mortgage companies and banks scrutinise every last piece of data to make sure they're lending on a property they can get their money back should the buyer default on their mortgage.

They need to be sure of the value the property is being sold.

Which means surveyors will not sign off on a property's value if they can't find evidence of an agent's claims…

It's more than their job's worth.

If an agent can't prove what other properties similar to yours have sold for, your potential buyer and their lender will down-value your property.

The reality for most sellers is having to continually climb mountains with no end in sight. The below illustration is the reality for most sellers when selling…

'The Reality...'

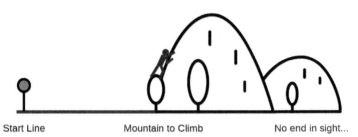

| Start Line | Mountain to Climb | No end in sight... |

Put another way, if a lender doesn't have comparable evidence confirming your property is worth what the buyer has agreed to pay, they may still offer a mortgage, but not at the level a buyer needs it to be in order to proceed which rarely ends well for sellers.

So you want proof that what the agent is telling you is tangible.

Think like a surveyor thinks.

The current rule of thumb that surveyors work with…

Completed properties (similar to yours) sold within the last 6 months and within a mile radius of your property.

In the meantime, check out these property websites if you haven't already seen them. Loads of valuable information.

www.getagent.co.uk

www.home.co.uk

www.homesearch.co.uk

INSIDER QUESTION #8

"How will local, national and international economies affect the sale of my property...?"

The simple answer is...

==>A lot.

Many economies and sectors will affect the sale of your home, not just your local area.

At an international level, it could be oil & gas, money markets, international elections, politics, natural disasters, war...

Nationally, you might have the High Speed 2 rail link tunnelling directly under your home...

Maybe planning permission has just been granted for 1000 new properties to be built on your doorstep over the next 7 to 10 years.

British Steel going into administration, or the state of car manufacturing will also affect the sale of your home.

Does the agent you're talking to know the answers to these questions?

Fact is...

All the above has the potential to negatively affect the sale of your home.

These are the exact same questions your potential buyers will be asking including their solicitor, the bank of mum and dad, terry down the pub, Amelie in the office...

Everyone will have an opinion.

If you've done your homework and the agent tries to bullsh*t you, how will they be representing you?

Make sure you take the time to study unrelated markets including what's happening at home and abroad.

Any agent that doesn't share this information with you is either negligent or worse, they don't know.

Remember...

Information is power.

And having this information will empower you irrespective of negative or potential scary information that comes to light before or during your house sale.

INSIDER QUESTION #9

"Mr Agent, what questions do you ask buyers to be absolutely confident they will make me an offer before they come to my home...?"

As I mentioned above, when I first started in the industry, I got more complaints than offers.

I literally got everything wrong, and my colleagues hovered over me like vultures...

I cringe now, but back then I'd ask buyers questions like what they did for a living or how much deposit they had...

My questioning had nothing to do with their dreams or aspirations.

I found out the hard way that knowing how much deposit a buyer has, has never and never will have an impact on selling a client's home.

Asking 'details' questions like 'do they have a deposit?' or whether they have a solicitor' are questions agents should want the answer to, but agents make buyers feel like they're being interrogated.

I was regularly pissing people off by asking stupid questions that nothing to do with a buyer's dreams...

Which lead to another nasty side effect.

I was unable to give sellers' any real feedback; other than the potential buyer did a viewing and didn't like the curtains or the colours of the wall weren't right.

Imagine I brought a potential buyer to your home and all I could tell you was that the buyers are from Basildon. They work and have a deposit of 20% and a mortgage in principle.

Compared to…

"One of the couples coming to view your home (Sally and David) have just missed out on a property exactly like yours. However, from the pictures and floorplan, your home looks like it could work better for them and their two children.

Not just that, your kitchen is pretty much the perfect size which means they don't have to extend.

Their kids are young, so being on a no-through road works perfectly.

They're currently in rented accommodation on a month's notice so should your property work for them, they'll be happy to work with you re-timings as they know you haven't found your new home yet."

In real life, I'd get a lot more information about what they want than above.

But, the more information about a person's reasons 'why' they want to view your home, the more likely they will make you an offer.

For example, what was the purpose of the buyer's call?

Let me be clear.

I wouldn't accept a buyer being shown my home if all the information the agent could get from them was that they had a job and were from Basildon.

Neither should you.

When agents are qualifying buyers, they should be building a buyer profile based on…

1) **Why this buyer?**

2) **Why your home?**

Not every buyer will offer. But the more the agent knows, the more likely a buyer will offer.

The point I'm making...

If an agent starts 'erming' and 'arghing' when you ask this question, it means they don't have a predictable and profitable process of qualifying buyers…

'Erming' and 'arghing' must be shown the door.

INSIDER QUESTION #10

"Who will be responsible for updating me on viewing feedback and deal progression once I'm under offer...?

Most of the time, the person responsible for updating the seller is the negotiator whose buyer (also known as an *Applicant*), won the right to buy a seller's home.

But…

What if this is the negotiator's first job out of school?

What if the agency they're working for doesn't educate their employees on the process of buying and selling houses?

What if their training consists of, "There's a desk. There's a phone. Get on the calls…"

In other words, they're 'learning on your dime…'

But when it comes to selling someone's property, 'learning on a sellers dime or learning on the job' is like giving a 17-year-old babysitter permission to take your £10 million vintage Ferrari out for a ride without a licence…

Literally.

That's who you could end up trusting to be in control of your most prized asset...

The person responsible for giving you feedback doesn't have to be the director or owner of the business, or even a manager.

But it must be someone who has a provable track record of results of keeping entire chains together and getting deals across the finish line.

There will be so many people involved in getting the sale of your property through to completion, from other agents to solicitors, to mortgage brokers, and each with varying skill levels.

Not only does the office neg (negotiator) representing you have to project manage all of the above personalities, they've also gotto manage an entire chain of properties.

But maybe the negotiator who's just started out will be struggling to hold their own hand, let alone being able to guide others in the chain of a thousand links.

Put another way, the person dealing with your sale must play many roles.

Mother. Father. Counsellor. Teacher. Estate Agent. Hostage Negotiator. Sage…

Said differently…

If they don't have skill and experience, they'll get eaten alive.

Not just by the thousand links in the chain, but by their colleagues. By their boss. By other sellers. Buyers. Solicitors. By the process and other peoples systems which will lead to overwhelm first. Then procrastination. Then they'll stop answering your calls.

The list goes on.

So the answer to this question is: make sure you're 100% certain the person looking after you either has bags of provable skill experience of successfully selling houses through previous client testimonials.

PS. at the very minimum, they should be updating you once per week whether you're under offer or not and many more times in-between.

INSIDER QUESTION #11

"What are your sole agency fees...?"

Would you work for £100 per month? Could you afford to work for £100 per month?

Circa 2016, I had won an instruction to sell a small mid terraced cottage.

Admittedly, I wasn't the first agent to be instructed. I wasn't even the second agent. Actually, I was the last agent the seller asked...

I was a last-ditch attempt to sell her home after months spent stagnating on the market with the entire high street of agents, but me..

And those agents were all too willing to take her property on, but none, it seemed, had the guts to tell her the truth...

Her problem was that she was relying on agents who were relying on luck.

Her next problem was that she had found her dream home. A property that was slipping from her hands as she was unable to sell hers.

It had been almost a year to the day when the office I was working for valued her property. £60,000 less than the agent she went with at £485,000

The good news for her was that the agent had found a buyer at £485,000.

Which of course fell through when the buyer realised they agreed to pay far too much for it.

The problem now.

She was **'Anchored'** to the £485,000 and based every subsequent financial decision and consideration around £485,000.

(google the anchoring effect. It's not pleasant and has a huge negative impact in this industry)

When this seller re-engaged with us, she struggled to give us her property saying, *"not only are your fees double the other agents (2%), you said my home was worth much less!"*

She had a point. Our fees WERE double what the other agents were charging and our marketing price WAS a lot less.

It didn't make sense to her.

But for her sake, I had to be blunt, "I don't say things that sound nice to win instructions. I've not promised my wife a holiday nor do I fear my boss on Monday morning if I don't win your instruction."

Sounds harsh, but my mission is to protect home sellers from Charlatans selling snake oil and pipe dreams.

In the end, we sold her cottage for £395,000.

If the original agents had eventually sold it, they would have billed 1% (less VAT) = £3950.

Happy days...

The original agents were a household-name that promoted themselves as **"achievers of superior results"**

In the end, she sold for £30,000 less than the £425,000 she should have got.

And of the £3950 in fee's, the negotiator if she had sold through the other high street agents, will have earnt £395 before tax.

Here's the thing.

Let's say the timeframe between going to market and completing takes 6 months…

It would have meant the negotiator would have been paid £65 per month.

Yes… I get it, The neg would be paid a salary too.

Would an expert in the sale of property be worth more than £65 per month to represent a seller's biggest asset?

You can't be the best agent in the area and charge the lowest fee…

But the agents claiming to be the best but charging the lowest fee isn't the best agent.

And if they can't protect their own fee, will they have the determination and courage to protect the marketing price they've told you?

So here's the truth, the higher an agent's valuation is and the closer their fee is to zero, the less likely they don't have a blueprint, a process or formula for maximising a seller's profits.

But they will have the systems and processes to win instructions plus cheap office labour to make sure the business owner wins, not you.

An agent whose valuation accuracy rate is at or very slightly below 100% is a 2% percent agent.

INSIDER QUESTION #12

"Do you insist all your clients have their property professionally photographed...?"

Imagine British soldiers went off to fight a modern war with pitchforks.

That'll be like using a Kodak to take marketing pictures of your home or worse, an agent standing in the corner of your front room attempting to take pictures with his blackberry...

You could have the worst looking home or the most stunning looking home. Either way, your property needs to be seen in its best light which is where professional photography comes in.

Interestingly, pro photography isn't for you. Pro photography is for your potential buyers...

It's for their friends. Their Colleagues. Their Solicitor. Their Lender. The lender's surveyor, the bank of Mum and Dad.

You need to make all of the above love your home when you come to sell.

Everyone else connected through work or friendship needs to be just as excited and enthusiastic as your buyer.

And if they're not.

It's because the pictures are poor.

And if the property details the agent produce is poor that'll equal no offer.

Not because the buyer doesn't want your home. It'll be because of negative peer pressure from the people around them.

And that would be a shame right…

Professional photography in estate agency is a minimum 50% of the battle in achieving a successful sale.

It means as much as that.

Sounds mental, but pro photography is a must.

Don't take any sh*t from an agent that says otherwise.

Even if they say they've completed a course in photography or have an amazing camera.

Get them to use professional Pro photography.

INSIDER QUESTION #13

"What strategy does your agency employ to maximise the value of the properties on your books...?"

Straight off the bat, if an agent doesn't tell you their strategy that maximises the value of their client's property, be afraid. Be very afraid.

Because without a strategy your property won't be perceived as one of a kind. It'll look like everything else on the market.

When valuing and discussing how to maximise the value of a client's home, being open with a seller about what I really think, especially if it's going to be seen as a negative, is a hard thing to do.

Most agents don't want to offend, so they choose popularity over having the guts to say what's right...

And the problem with being popular, it costs homeowners thousands of pounds.

When I'm valuing a seller's home, I ask them, **"How are you going to get every potential buyer to stop what they're doing and get them to come to your home instead?"**

In other words...

If you can accept your property is 100% in competition with other similar properties on the market, you will achieve maximum results every time....

Ask the agent what their strategy is?

Do they have a strategy that they can demonstrate that consistently achieves superior results against their competitors?

INSIDER QUESTION #14

"In your opinion, what is the value of my property? And can you provide comparable evidence of actual and recently sold properties supporting your valuation...?"

With this question, you're beginning to reveal the **skilled agent versus the unskilled agent.**

The **ethical agent versus the unethical agent.**

The **integrity-driven agent versus those with a lack of integrity.**

If the agent you're speaking to does not (or cannot) provide evidence to confirm what he's saying, he's bullsh*tting you in an attempt to use your home to keep his office doors open as opposed to using his agency to open doors for you.

Equally, if he or she is able to show you evidence backing up their valuation with a good number of property details, then perfect! They're not bullsh*tting you.

Remember. 6 months. 1 mile radius.

But...

Do not be fooled by an *"on the market"* price. You need to see actual sold prices within the last 6 months within a 1-mile radius.

Remember, only properties sold within the last 6 months and within a mile of your property will be considered proof by Surveyors.

On a TikTok Live, I was asked what is the single killer question to ask estate agents at a valuation?

There are actually 4.

1. **"How much is my property worth...?"**
2. **"How much do you suggest I market my property for...?"**
3. **"What price will get the 10 very best buyers round to my home right now…?"**
4. **"If you won my instruction, will you sell my property for free should you fail to deliver on your price promise...?"**

The price difference between question 1 and 3 shouldn't be different and the agent that says they'll absolutely sell your house for free (#4) is the agent who's being must truthful and the one that you can trust.

INSIDER QUESTION #15

"Can you tell me exactly how many buyers you have actively looking for a property like mine at the price point you've suggested...?"

If you were with me, we were 10 minutes away from jumping into the unknown. Tensions. Aggression. The blokes became more and more violent in their attempts to find an inch of space in the packed fuselage of an RAF C-130 Hercules...

I was part of an entire battle group of a thousand men taking part in a three-week exercise in Scotland.

We weren't being taken there by wheels on a bus.

We were jumping at 130mph from 243 meters above the ground.

Most of the blokes at that time were already battle-hardened from tours such as Kosovo and Sierra Leonne.

Yet, these robust battle-hardened soldiers were vomiting into sick bags...

Not only that, but we were also exiting the aircraft with 180lbs of equipment strapped to us.

Looking out the portside door I was the 22nd man in the door, allowing me to see two other Hercules

C-130's with their first men in their door's looking back at us.

It was like a scene from a film.

The plane rose to 800ft.

The RED light came to life…

5 seconds later, "GREEN ON…!"

GO! GO! GO!

In rapid succession, paratroopers were exiting the aircraft one after the other…

By this time, I had done 13 jumps in my army career and was a little more worried than normal.

My worry wasn't jumping.

My worry was missing the Drop Zone.

Missing the Drop Zone by just a few seconds in a plane doing 130mph meant landing a lifetime away from where we should have been dropped. Especially having to carry 180Ibs!

Half the blokes had managed to get out the door, then suddenly, the plane lost power.

The blokes that were still on the plane including myself were thrown all over the place.

Yet the Loadmaster at the door was still screaming GO! GO! GO!

Somehow I made it out the door…

ONE THOUSAND. TWO THOUSAND. THREE THOUSAND. CHECK CANOPY…

As soon as my chute opened, I saw the sky below was filled with paratroopers that jumped about 10 to 15 seconds before my wave.

As I looked up, another wave of paratroopers exited their aircraft.

At that moment there were well over 1000 chutes in the sky.

Just like a brigade jump, buyers also come in waves.

Wave One: Agents should have at least five to seven buyers actively looking for a property like yours at the price point they've told you.

Wave Two: These are buyers the agent doesn't know. They're actively looking but will only raise their hand if they agree with the marketing price.

Wave Three. If you're relying on this wave of buyers, you'll have a serious problem as these buyers may not even turn up at all.

Let me explain.

Before an agent comes to your home, they already know who on their books is likely to make you an offer (That is of course if they've qualified their buyers properly), which may be just one or two buyers which is fine.

So, if they tell you they have seven buyers lined up and only two people come to view your home in the first week and you don't get an offer, the agent has over-valued your property.

Thing is...

The sale of your home must be on your terms and you must attract all three waves of buyers to your home at the same time.

So...

"Mr agent, how many buyers do you have actively looking for a property like mine at the price point you've told me?"

If they don't know the exact number that's a little bit of a problem.

But if they then fail to tell you what I've just told you above about the three waves of buyers, then they're selling you a lengthy contract...

INSIDER QUESTION #16

"Is your valuation the figure I'm likely to achieve...?"

Now we're getting to the heart of whether agent has integrity or not, as this question is designed to the give the agent no room for manoeuvre, because they've already giving a figure in **INSIDER QUESTION #14.**

The answer is a simple YES or NO?

If they say "hmmm, well, erm…" you will have just freaked them out and you'll have discovered whether they're really that confident about the first figure they gave you?

Remember all these questions are designed to put you in total control of the sale of your home, not the agent.

The agent that truly has your best interests at heart is the difference between an amateur focusing on making sales versus a professional focusing on building relationships.

If they're full of sh*t, this question will reveal it

However, saying yes does not get them off the hook just yet.

INSIDER QUESTION #17

"On average, how many competing offers per property do you generate for your clients' properties...?"

Creating a situation where there are competing offers on every property is nowhere near guaranteed, but it's the target all agents should be looking to achieve for their sellers.

Always!

In the previous question they confirmed to you the price you should sell for.

Okay, cool.

Now let them show you the evidence of how many competing offers they generate...

Agents should have a library of stats from the number of viewings they achieve per property, to how many people they called about it. How many buyers offered on each of their properties to the price it sold for compared against the price it was marketed at.

They should use this information to spot trends in their local market.

You'll want to see this information too.

This information is key for two reasons.

1. To clearly understand exactly how much your property is worth and
2. selling for more than your property is worth.

To truly sell for much more than the market value, you need to get buyers to compete.

And to achieve this, properties need to be bang on the money with their marketing price.

The fact is, you don't need competing offers to achieve the asking price.

The reason you want competing offers is not just to give you the ability to achieve over the asking price for your home, but also to make sure if your property sale falls out of bed with one buyer you can easily replace with the next buyer…

In other words,

…you can replace the sale without losing a wink of sleep…

Only if the property is priced correctly, positioned properly and the genet understands consumer psychology.

INSIDER QUESTION #18

"How many weeks is your minimum term contract, and does it contain a notice period...?"

77 days after accepting an offer, the agent finally admitted the buyer he introduced couldn't get a mortgage!

Steve, a friend of mine from my Parachute Regiment days, was furious.

He and his wife were spending lots of money on solicitors fees. Mortgage fees and various other surveys in an attempt to buy their dream home.

Yet for almost three months their buyer still wasn't in a position to proceed which it transpired; the agent knew about.

Steve had pretty much done what everyone else connected with the sale had asked him to do...

He told me, "My missus wanted an explanation from him (the agent) as to why the buyers were allowed to go 11 weeks without being picked up for no mortgage?"

The agent told her it was not his responsibility! But in fact, it was the buyer's solicitor's responsibility to inform Steve...

WHAT... THE...!

Point to note if this happens to you.

This is not the job of the solicitor. And even if it was, the agent should be all over it regardless...

So many times, sales have unnecessarily fallen out of bed because agents are not checking whether a buyer is proceedable (a buyer with a mortgage in principle doesn't make them proceedable) leaving sellers to miss out on their dream homes because of lacklustre 'can't be arsed' performance...

Equally, the agent dealing with the sale doesn't know what they're doing.

The point I'm making...

When Steve tried to dis-instruct his agent, they enforced a 28-day notice period.

W...T...F...!

They literally failed to chase or mention that Steve's buyer did not have a mortgage for 11 weeks, yet felt they were entitled to get paid?

The agent locked Steve and his wife into the contract!?

To be clear, it's the agent's job to make sure everybody involved knows what's going on at all times from the first to the last link in the chain.

...and I mean everyone.

The point I'm making. Don't sign a contract that lasts more than 30 days.

A 30-day contract is long enough.

10 to 12-week contracts are designed to keep you locked in so you can't go anywhere else enabling an agent to beat you down on their deliberate over estimation later...

Good agents will have no problem with a 30-day contract.

Why?

Because they understand exactly what they're doing.

and I can't stress this enough, a correctly priced property under offer within a matter of weeks of coming to market.

Said differently...

Don't be the seller that finds themselves in Steve's position that you cannot get out of.

On the contract, write 30 days and cross out the 28 day notice period and get the agent to sign the page to acknowledge what they've agreed.

INSIDER QUESTION #19

"When a buyer makes me an offer, how will your estate agency present it to me...?"

Imagine for a moment, you've been told, "You know the most amazing couple who viewed your home on Saturday. The couple in the most incredible buying position... Well... they are going to make you an offer!"

You were assured they were so perfect; you accepted their offer and excitedly called your other half to tell them the news.

You employed a highly recommended solicitor.

You paid your lender to carry out a full structural survey on your dream purchase...

A week passed and you're still waiting for news on when your buyers' survey is taking place.

Three weeks have now passed, and your buyer's solicitor still hasn't asked your solicitor a single question. Yet your solicitor is flying - the searches are back, and a written mortgage offer is in the post.

Five weeks have now passed, and you've been told that the buyer has paid for their survey, but it still hasn't been booked in.

Meanwhile, the buyer's solicitor still hasn't been in contact with yours????

Where's your agent?!

Your agent should be showing you proof that anyone offering really are in a position to proceed.

So what do you need to see?

- Firstly, confirmation in writing (letter or email) from the buyer's lender that they have a mortgage in principle. (MIP's mean nothing by the way. Not the buyer's fault. It just shows the buyer has taken the time to speak to a lender.)

- Confirmation in writing from the buyer's solicitor that they have been instructed to act on the buyer's behalf.

- Actual proof that your potential buyer has the required deposit. i.e. cash in the bank. Not money tied up in a vague investment fund.

- Confirmation in writing from the buyer that they can work to your timeframes to complete the sale.

Why would the Agent show you all of this?

Because your agent works for you and if they are managing the sale properly, (especially if it is part of a chain) their role is to make sure all parties across the entire chain are aware of progress and agree to work to deadlines.

Selling your home is a project.

If your agent isn't in control of the project, then you're not.

The agent you employ is responsible for making sure you get the highest possible price, but their first priority should be protecting your future by making sure the person you've agreed to sell to (based on all the evidence presented) will and can work towards your timeframes.

Not being shown the details above is as good as your agent taking you hiking across Dartmoor in the dark and without a torch.

They'll get you lost and your sale will die.

INSIDER QUESTION #20

"How many testimonials can you show me for you personally including members of your office team…?"

Most high street agencies look great on the outside.

Modern. Fresh. Exciting.

There are some Agencies that from the outside look dishevelled, battered and broken. Paint peeling off the walls including letters missing from the company logo.

Some agents don't even have an office.

Which of the three types of agents above would you use?

Modern, battered or no office?

What if you were thinking of using 'modern and fresh' only to discover 'battered and broke' achieved more superior results…

What if 'battered and broke's average asking price achieved for their homeowners was higher than all of their competition?

What if their clients' properties were snapped up immediately for over the asking price?

What if they expertly put their clients in total control of the selling process?

How would you know?

The point I'm making is this.

Whether the agent looks fresh and exciting or battered and broken, the question to any agent should be, *"can you show me what people are saying about your agency and what they're saying about you and the individual negotiators inside your office?"*

After all, how would you know if the agent's you interview only skillset was the ability to talk a good game?

Agents with nothing to hide would happily show you proof of what people were saying about them.

The point I'm making, if you want to be as sure as you can about the agents you're talking to, it's a completely necessary question to ask.

INSIDER QUESTION #21

"Should you not deliver on your promises including delivering the figure you said I should expect to achieve, will your agency sell my property for free...?"

Should agents face consequences for poor or misleading advice...? i.e., should they get paid if they fail to deliver their price promise?

I believe they should sell your home for FREE if they don't deliver on their promises.

Why?

Because agents know exactly what a property is worth. The pros will have the honesty to tell you. 99% won't.

As I've said earlier in the book; the value of a property is not subjective. If it was, banks and mortgage companies would lend on everything, but they do not.

Imagine an agent that looked you in the eyes and promised you what he said was real, but after a month of poor performance his only solution was to push YOU to drop the price?

In my opinion, that would be like paying a bricklayer who failed to build you a wall but told you owed them more for the lack of progress.

Or a cab driver who failed to deliver you to the destination you asked to go.

Would you pay them?

I wouldn't either.

Yet, based on poor performance figures (price reductions) we see online, how many agencies get away with non-performance?

All of them…

It's common practice.

But what if an agent guaranteed you that if they failed to deliver on their promises, they would sell your home for free?!

I would love this to be enshrined in legislation. I want it to be an industry wide standard.

I believe there should always be consequences in any business that fail to deliver what they've promised the consumer.

But especially in this industry.

Without consequences, unethical agents will continue to sacrifice sellers for their own gain.

And this is why this question is so powerful.

Because with all said and done, this question reveals the truth of what an agent really thinks despite all of the answers they've given you above.

"CLOSING THOUGHTS..."

Here's the thing...

Before you go to market.

Before you even dare sign a contract.

You have to ask Estate Agents these questions.

The reason you're asking these questions is that you are trying to discover the difference between the professionals, and the amateurs that say things that sound nice...

All these questions are designed to deliberately attach an emotional consequence to their actions.

In other words, if they don't deliver on everything, they've told you, what are their self-imposed consequences?

The agent that says, "If I don't deliver on the price point, I've made you, I will sell your property for free..." They're taking maximum responsibility for their actions...

And the agent that starts telling you a story, "argh well you know..." who starts spinning you a yarn of "If, buts, maybe's, when's, whys."

Then he or she has just told you the story of how they see the sale going at the price point they've just told you…

Remember your house sale is about you.

Not the agent.

There are some fantastic agents out there.

You're now armed with the questions that'll reveal them.

"WHAT NOW...?"

"Sell Your Property with Confidence - My Price Promise Guarantee Ensures Your Satisfaction..."

Don't settle for less - trust me to get you the best possible price for your home, backed by my 100% price guarantee. If I don't deliver on my price promise, I'll sell your home for free...

Dear friend,

Are you looking to sell your home quickly and at the best possible price?

I understand that selling your home can be a daunting task, but I'm here to make the process easy and stress-free...

I believe in offering home sellers the best possible service, which is why I'm proud to offer a 100% price guarantee. That's right - I guarantee that I will sell your home for exactly what I say I will, or I will sell your property for free.

As an experienced and dedicated estate agent, I will work tirelessly to ensure that your home is sold quickly and efficiently marketing your property through a variety of channels, including online listings, social media that attracts the very best buyers. I will also provide you with regular updates on the status of your sale, so you never feel out of the loop.

I understand that selling your home can be a stressful time, which is why I offer a personalised approach for each of my clients. I will work with you to understand your unique needs and goals and create a tailored sales strategy that meets those needs.

So why choose my estate agency? My 100% price guarantee is just one of the many reasons. I am committed to providing you with the best possible service, and I will not stop until you are completely satisfied with the outcome of your sale.

Don't settle for less when it comes to selling your home. Choose me and let me help you get the price you deserve. Contact me today to schedule a consultation on 07407 232 619 or john@savageandsavage.co.uk

Sincerely,

John Savage - Managing Director

Savage & Savage

Printed in Great Britain
by Amazon